Lets
TAKE IT
to the
MAT

SHOOT!

TAKE YOUR SHOT!

SPRAWL!

BELLY DOWN!

STAND UP!

HE'S PINNED!

SHORT TIME!

SHOOT!

TAKE YOUR SHOT!

SPRAWL!

STAND UP!

BELLY DOWN!

HE'S PINNED!

SHORT TIME!

Washington, Gregory T.

Getting the Win

ISBN:

Hard Cover - 978-1-7356993-1-8

Paperback- 978-1-7356993-2-5

E-book - 978-1-7356993-3-2

This book is dedicated to my children and every child that has ever faced a challenging time in their life.

No matter how difficult the challenge may be, always pick yourself back up and take another shot at your goal! You got this, just believe in yourself! You are Made to Win!

MADE TO WIN!

WELCOME TO MIDDLE SCHOOL
SPORTS SIGN-UP

Wrestling
When: Wednesday at 2:30 pm
Where: Room N154
Coach: Coach T

Football
When: Thursday at 2:30 pm
Where: N201
Coach: Coach Taylor

Basketball
When: Monday at 2:30 pm
Where: Room N129
Coach: Coach Peterson

Track
When: Tuesday at 2:30 pm
Where: Room N100
Coach: Coach Chambers

Soccer
When: Thursday at 2:30 pm
Where: N101
Coach: Coach O'Donnell

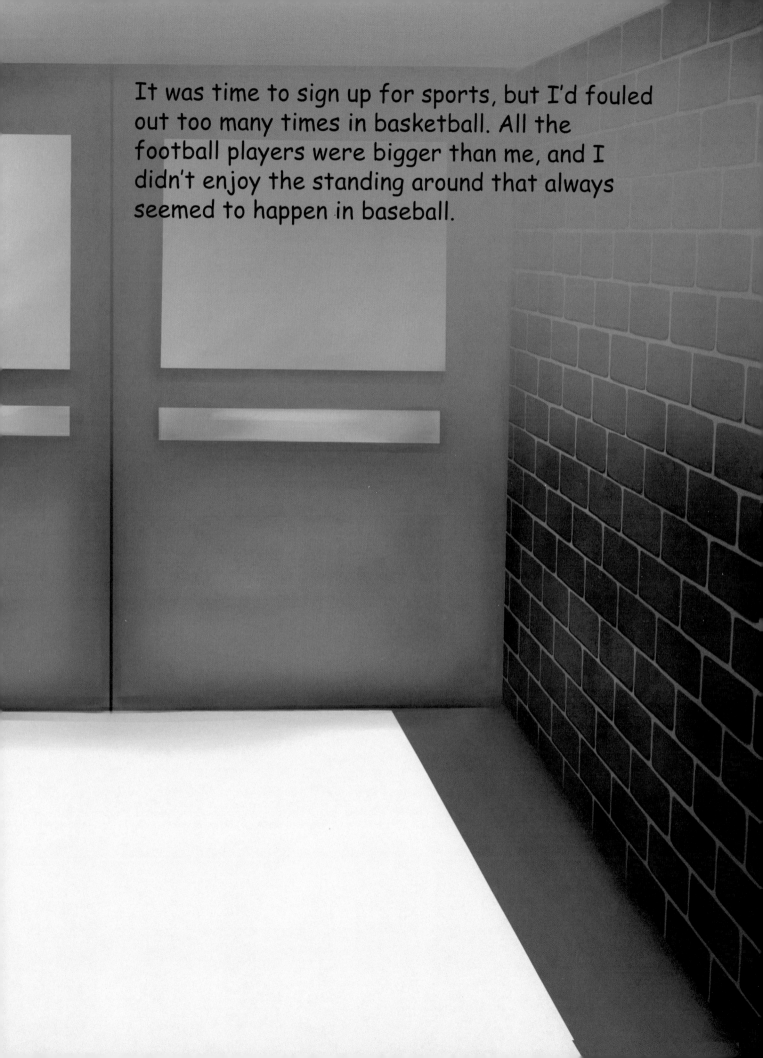

It was time to sign up for sports, but I'd fouled out too many times in basketball. All the football players were bigger than me, and I didn't enjoy the standing around that always seemed to happen in baseball.

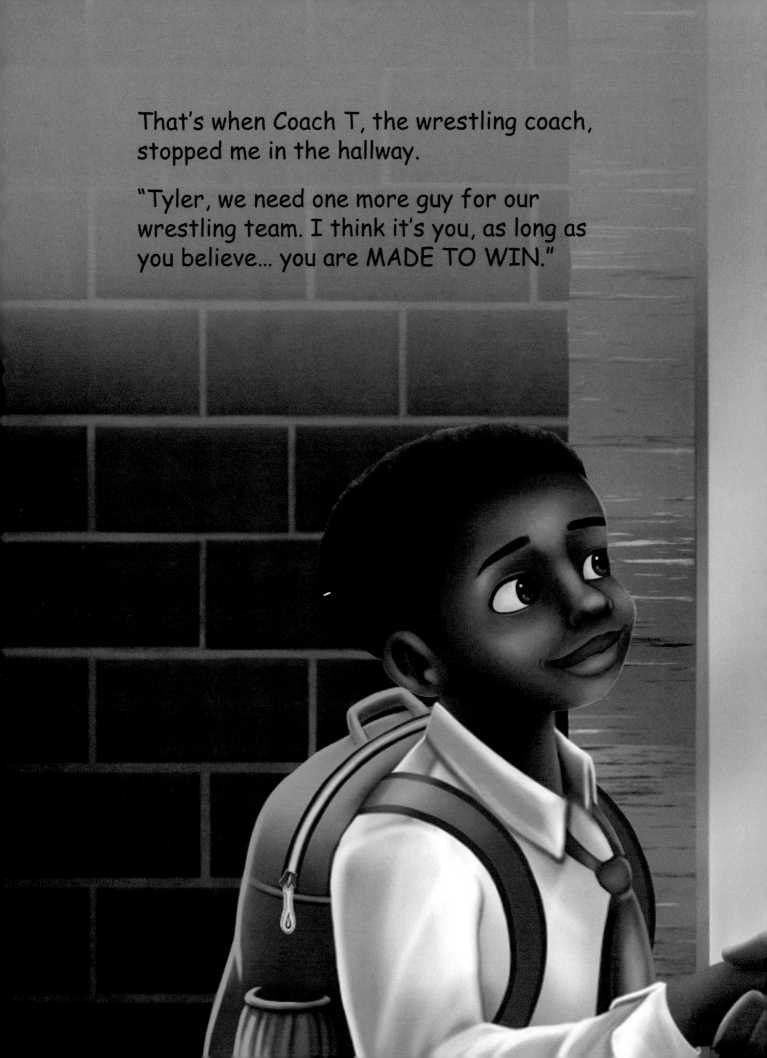

That's when Coach T, the wrestling coach, stopped me in the hallway.

"Tyler, we need one more guy for our wrestling team. I think it's you, as long as you believe... you are MADE TO WIN."

Although I was nervous, I decided to give wrestling a try. After all, Coach T thought I might be the right guy so I had to at least make an attempt.

On the first day of practice, Coach T asked us to repeat his favorite phrase. As loud as we could, we repeated, "I WAS MADE TO WIN. I PREPARE TO WIN. EVERY DAY IS A NEW DAY TO WIN!"

I said it even though I wasn't sure I believed it. However, as I continued to practice, Coach T shouted near me, "When I was your age, I lost all my matches because I had a negative attitude. Do you have a negative attitude, Tyler?"

As the season continued, my attitude started to morph. The thought of wrestling mats on the gym floor instantly gave me a rush. It made me feel like I was training for the Olympics, stepping out of my comfort zone and into a newly improved me!

Some days I wanted to give up, but I couldn't. Hearing my teammates yelling, "I WAS MADE TO WIN. I PREPARE TO WIN. EVERY DAY IS A NEW DAY TO WIN!" helped me believe this sport is my win.

As the wrestling season continued, I lost match after match. I started to doubt myself. Maybe this sport was NOT my win. I kept getting pinned, and it was difficult to keep a winning attitude.

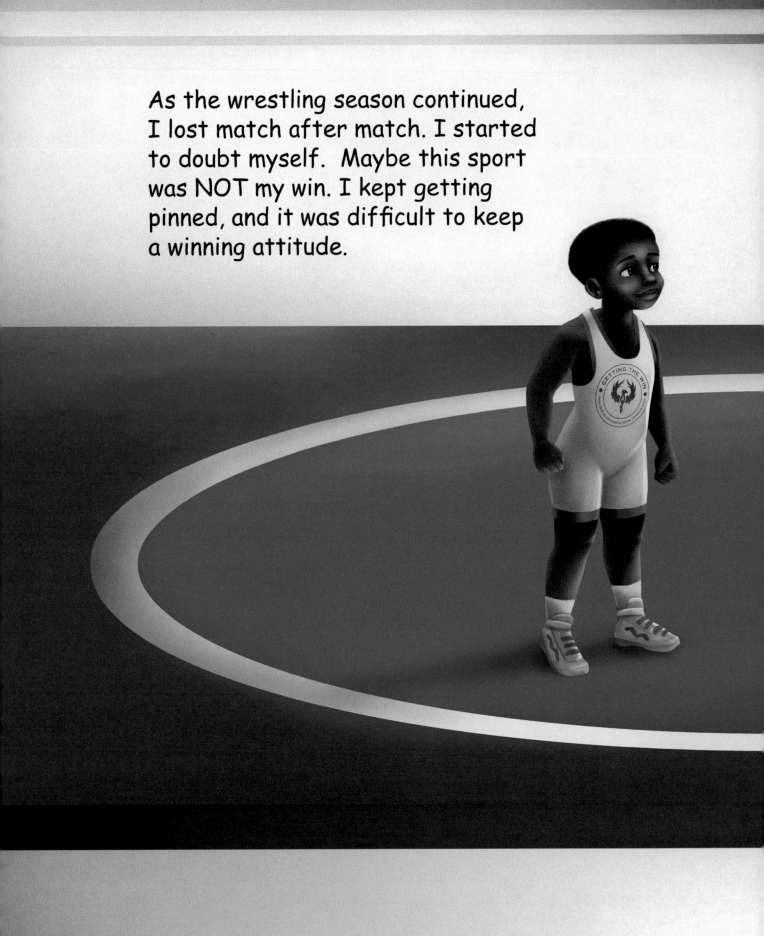

Coach T gave me tips at practice to help me stay off my back. When he yelled, "BELLY DOWN," that meant to immediately put your belly to the mat.

Practices were hard...the hardest thing
I have ever done! My practice shirt and
shorts were always drenched in sweat.
They were so wet, I looked as if I had
just come out of the pool.

The next match came, and I believed I was ready. After a tough loss in overtime, I walked off the mat with my head down and eyes flooded with tears.

Coach T said with a strong, stern voice, "Pick your head up! The way you walk off the mat represents your character. You come from greatness; let's walk like it and act like it!"

I picked up my head and didn't give up. I decided to go back to practice, even though I was worried that I would never win a match.

After practice, Coach T talked to the team, but it felt as if he was speaking directly to me. "Next week is our last match and, as you can see, success doesn't come overnight. It's a process, and you must believe and trust YOUR process."

"Each day when you tell yourself you are MADE TO WIN, I need you to believe it because it's what got you through the challenging times all season. You were dedicated both on and off the mat." Then we all chanted together: "I WAS MADE TO WIN. I PREPARE TO WIN. EVERY DAY IS A NEW DAY TO WIN!"

I took Coach T's advice and even ran after practice each day before my last match. I ate healthy and practiced strengthening my technique. I started to set goals for myself and worked hard to reach them. I now believed I WAS MADE TO WIN!

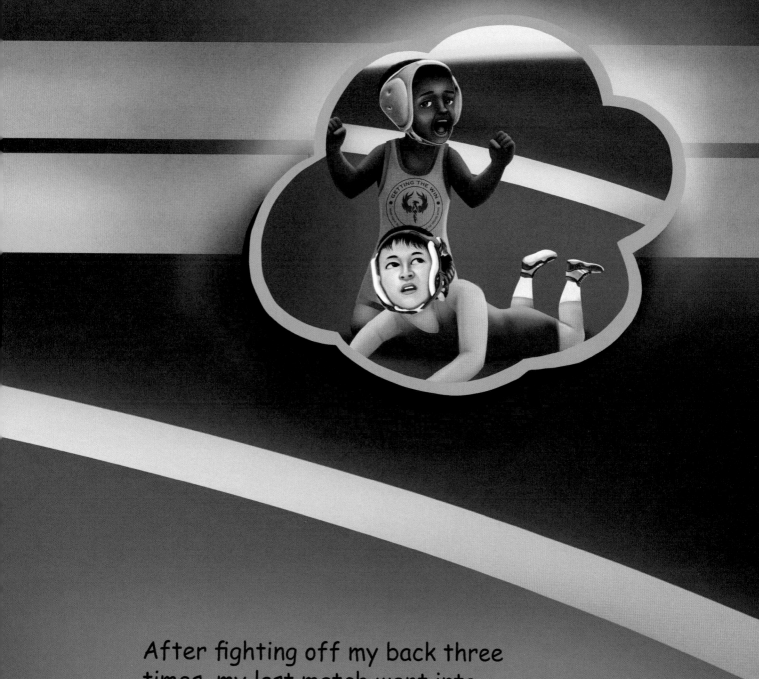

After fighting off my back three times, my last match went into overtime. When the whistle blew to start overtime, I took a deep breath and launched into my favorite take down—a double leg takedown!

And, I did it! I took him down to win the match! I was so excited that I couldn't stop smiling.

After walking off the mat, I humbly thanked my coach, my team, and my family for their support in my new lifestyle of wrestling. My worst days were my best days because they prepared me for today—the best day ever!

MADE TO WIN!

RUN THE HALF

SHOOT!

TAKE YOUR SHOT!

SPRAWL!

BELLY DOWN!

STAND UP!

HE'S PINNED!

SHORT TIME!

RUN THE HALF

SHOOT!

TAKE YOUR SHOT!

SPRAWL!

BELLY DOWN!

STAND UP!

HE'S PINNED!

SHORT TIME!

Made in the USA
Middletown, DE
12 December 2023

45438911R00024